Hycel's Story

Hycel Lee Peterson and
Kenneth Bernard Peterson

Xulon Press

Xulon Press
2301 Lucien Way #415
Maitland, FL 32751
407.339.4217
www.xulonpress.com

Scripture quotations taken from the King James Version (KJV)—*public domain.*

Printed in the United States of America.

ISBN-13: 9781545609668

ACKNOWLEDGMENTS

*M*y nephew Ken and I would like to thank all of the many people who have assisted us with the writing of this book. No matter how small a part you think you may have played, there is no possible way we get this book written without your help.

Although too many to name individually without running the risk of forgetting someone who contributed, we do want to mention certain key individuals without whom there would be no story to tell. This includes all of my family members including my mother Mary Peterson and my father Eddie Percival Peterson. My school teachers who were also my Aunts, Inez Lowe and Gertha Huching. Technician Training school and my instructor, Armand Petrucci. Mason Plastering of Pittsburgh, James Bass Contractors of Newark New Jersey and Nu Towne Construction also in New Jersey.

CHAPTER 1

$\mathcal{I}$ came across a copy of this letter, written by my Uncle Hycel Peterson almost 25 years ago, and as I began to read it... this uncle, whom I just begun to get to know over the past 20 years, revealed to me a part of "his story." This he did, while at the same time educating me concerning our family history thus answering a lot of questions concerning my own identity. What about my inherent qualities? Why do I have this propensity towards self-employment? Why did my dad drink the way he did? Why when my father drank did he always refer to himself as "Sargent Peterson?" Could some of those questions be answered by just learning more about my family history?

Uncle Hycel did not know this, but there has been for quite some time, a longing in my heart to know my family history particularly from my father's side. I knew my father migrated from the south, met and married my mother who was from Pittsburgh,

Pennsylvania, but that was the extent of it. Why did he come here? What made him the kind of man that I knew him to be- such a complicated man who at times seemed like an almost contradiction in terms. On the one hand, he was the hardest working, family-oriented Christian man I knew; but on the other hand, he had this problem with alcohol which seemed to make it impossible for him to take a social drink without spiraling into weeks of non-stop binge-drinking before returning to his normal responsible hard-working self. Many of these questions would be answered as I listened to my uncle speak.

I call him my favorite uncle; likewise, he calls me his favorite nephew. A builder by trade, he has described to me all of the projects he has been involved in over the past 80-plus years which I can tell by the radiance that suddenly appears over his countenance, that he is very proud of his accomplishments … As well he should be.

His letter starts out as a letter, but quickly unfolds as a story — his story, one that I have found quite compelling…

September 12, 2012

"Dear Mr. President:

I am writing to you because I believe what you are trying to do. My name is Hycel Lee Peterson and I am 61 years old. My father, Eddie Peterson, died in 1946. He was 41 years old. My mother, Mary Peterson turned 83 January 6th of this year.

My parents Eddie Percival Peterson and Mary Magdalene Peterson had seven children. When my father passed away eight months later, my mother gave birth to my baby brother Harold. Now there were eight of us ranging in ages from newborn to 18. We lived on a farm in which my father rented, in Randolph County Georgia. Our address was Rte. 1, Box 27, Springville, GA ..."

This letter which was written to then President Barrack Obama almost seems as though it is a cry for help. Apparently, this letter had been written and rewritten at various times as I rambled through his notes and found several copies with different dates. It would seem to me that my uncle, in his own way was bound and determined to tell his story.

After all these years having lived with this sense of injustice which wreaked havoc upon our family, it still has never been

3

made quite right in his eyes. "Well, maybe...just maybe...now that we have and African-American President, it can be made right," I could sense him saying.

"The audacity of hope," sometimes against all hope is all we need to keep us going. My uncle Hycel has never given up on the prospect that one day, these injustices would be made right. The pain is still there though, almost as real as it was from the beginning as he makes clear in the pages to follow.

"My grandfather, Charlie Peterson, owned a large piece of land," began Hycel as he began to unfold the mysteries that I have sought after and expounded upon our family's history. "As I was told by my aunts and uncles located in fertile Clay County in Georgia, during hard times, he was forced to mortgage his property. He was described as a wealthy man... His children were all well-educated, (especially for blacks during that time). I received my education from one of my aunts who had received a college education."

"Having mortgaged his property," he continued, "my grandfather tried repaying his debt by producing timber which he retrieved by cutting down some of the trees that were on his property. The bank, however, forbade him from cutting timber on the mortgaged property, thereby precipitating the foreclosure

4

of his land. In those days, if a black man owned something "they" wanted, (they meaning banks owned by corrupt businessman) they would find a way to get it either legally or Illegally."

"This same banking institution," he continued, "then went on to rent my grandfather one of its many other properties. This would become the place where he would continue to raise his family. Our newly-rented land was located approximately 25 miles south of our home which we often afterwards referred to as the "home place." The land was very fertile at the home Place, especially compared to our new property which was very rocky," continued Hycel.

We began to struggle it seems from that point on in our lives. My grandfather's health took a turn for the worse as he soon had a stroke not long after his property was stolen. One of his daughters, my Aunt Eva Peterson (Long), had a nervous breakdown. This was all a direct result of hardships brought about because of the many losses we suffered. My grandfather died not long after the stroke, unwittingly leaving his wife and children to fend for themselves.

Most of my aunts and uncles opted to stay on the newly-rented property after he died, however my father Eddie decided to leave Georgia and the awful racism that existed in the South in the year 1928 and move to Columbus, Ohio. It was short-lived, however, as soon afterward, my father began to experience financial hardship due to the state of the economy brought on by the great depression. And it was further complicated by the ever-increasing number of mouths to feed. Suddenly, it was time to head back to Georgia where at least my father could farm on my grandfather's rented land.

At that time, my parents had two children, and my mother was pregnant with the third. Both my grandparents passed not long after my parents returned to Georgia. My grandmother passed at childbirth, bearing twin girls which my parents helped raise. Reathel and Ruthel were my Aunts, but were raised alongside us like sisters. Together we became just one big happy family.

Everyone in the household would contribute to the farming. After the crops were laid, and the weeds were no longer a threat to them, my father would find work in the sawmill to supplement the household income. As a young man, I never understood how my father continued to do all he did. I later learned that that he had a deep abiding love for his family.

Keeping food on the table for seven children was a responsibility which kept my father busy. Additionally, he was also tasked with planning and preparing for any unforeseen needs to come. It required the help of someone supernatural. It required the help of the Lord. I am reminded of the scriptures in Psalms 121: 1 and 2 in which David declares,

1   I will lift up mine eyes unto the hills, from whence cometh my help.

2   My help cometh from the LORD, which made heaven and earth. (KJV)

Most of the blacks in our community were not able to attend school during the planting, cultivating and harvesting season due to the fact that they were sharecroppers. My parents, however, made sure we received an education by making us attend school anyhow. There were four families residing on this rented land. (All of us were related). I called it a village, because looking back, all the adults took part in raising all the children. In modern day language, whether near or far, I guess it really does "take a village to raise a child."

We all went to school together. Our school was one large room with a pot belly stove to keep us warm in the colder months. It was where children of all ages gathered together to get an education. My aunts were all teachers, and it often seemed to me that they were harder on me than they were on many of the other students. I understand now why, and I am grateful they didn't cut me slack just because my name was Peterson. Even with the education I have received, it has been difficult at best to maintain employment. I can't imagine how difficult it would have been had I not been educated and motivated by teachers such as my "Aunties" as I call them.

I was raised during a time when the parents trained up children using the wise counsel offered in the Scriptures ... Particularly "he that spares the rod hates his son (KJV)," located in the Proverbs of Solomon. Our parents were keenly aware of the importance of us having an education. I remember my summer vacation ending and my school year beginning much earlier than the other children in the community. Extra time was often needed for many of us to get in a disciplined frame of mind. Our parents encouraged the teachers to apply the "board of education" to the "seat of knowledge" lest we not take our education seriously. I can personally attest to the fact that they took heed to our parent's instruction.

When my father died of leukemia, I was only 14 years old. Although my oldest brother Eddie and sister Esther were away from home attending boarding school, my education was then put on hold because I had to go to work and support our family as every able-bodied male in the family did. At the time, there were

8

no social security benefits, and certainly no welfare benefits. So, Eddie and I began working at the same sawmill my father had previously worked at to help support the family. Although we were all devastated by the loss of our father, by the grace of God, in Whom we were taught to believe in from a child, we managed to survive.

At the age of 14, the work I was doing at the sawmill seemed extremely difficult for me. What started out as me carrying slabs of timber would often turn into me dragging slabs of timber as they seemed to get heavier and heavier by the minute. It felt like something in my back was tearing apart as I persisted against the pain to try and complete the task at hand.

Eddie Peterson

Esther Peterson (Humbert)

Hycel Lee Peterson

Kenneth James Peterson (KJ)

Bernice Peterson (Blackwell)

Sallie Peterson (Stevenson)

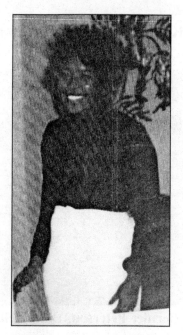

Shirley Ann Peterson

Harold Peterson

Eddie Percival Peterson

Mary Magdalene Peterson (Mama)

Quitting was never an option for me though, because none of my other brothers were old enough to work. Eventually, the pain would go away… Or so it seemed. Life was beginning to get back to normal a little while after my father passed. All the kids were in school, my brother Eddie and I were working at the sawmill and we were able to earn enough money to feed and clothe the entire family. Psalm 112 has always been my favorite scripture as it has given me strength and guidance through the years.

Psalms 112

1 Praise ye the Lord. Blessed is the man that feareth the Lord, that delighteth greatly in his commandments.

2 His seed shall be mighty upon earth: the generation of the upright shall be blessed.

3 Wealth and riches shall be in his house: and his righteousness endureth forever.

4 Unto the upright there ariseth light in the darkness: he is gracious, and full of compassion, and righteous.

5 A good man sheweth favour, and lendeth: he will guide his affairs with discretion.

6 Surely, he shall not be moved forever: the righteous shall be in everlasting remembrance.

7 He shall not be afraid of evil tidings: his heart is fixed, trusting in the Lord.

8 His heart is established, he shall not be afraid, until he see his desire upon his enemies.

9 He hath dispersed, he hath given to the poor; his righteousness endureth for ever; his horn shall be exalted with honour.

10 The wicked shall see it, and be grieved; he shall gnash with his teeth, and melt away: the desire of the wicked shall perish.

King James Version (KJV)

My brother and I worked every day just trying to keep our heads above water ... The rare exception being we were severely ill. Eddie was also responsible for driving the trucks which transported workers to and from the work site as well as transporting the logs. The logs were often loaded so heavily upon the truck that the front wheels of the truck would at times lift off the ground while the vehicle was in motion. I was afraid for him and spent many days praying for his safety. God was always with him.

However, Life as a kid was not always all work and no play. Because my brother had a car, he would occasionally take me to visit my girlfriend who lived on the other side of town. When I went to see Annie. He would drop me off and go visit his friends. He would pick me up by 11 PM (that is the time I had to be out. My girlfriend's family was strict regarding courtship rules). Sometimes, when he was late, I was put out and had to start trudging through the swamp alone because "visiting hours were over at Annie's Carl's house, and any and all male visitors must leave by 11 PM." That was the rule. That's also the way things were done back then. I had the utmost respect for Annie and her parents, and trudging through the swamp late at night was just a small price to pay to be with the one I loved.

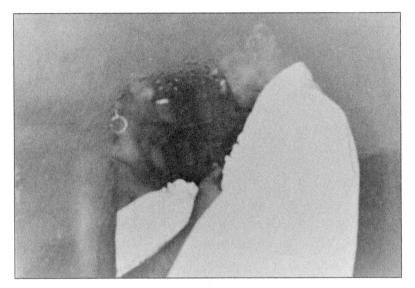

Hycel and first love Annie Pearl Rogers

As I Mentioned, all the kids were in school, my brother Eddie and I were working at the sawmill and could feed and clothe the whole family.

Although the work was extremely difficult, we were grateful for work of any kind. At times, it even seemed as though we were working in labor camps... As we were often "incidentally" given a "glimpse" of the pistol the boss carried around in his pocket. If a worker had to use the bathroom, and was gone in the bushes for longer than the boss deemed reasonable, he would be ordered out immediately to explain his delay. In the 1940s, that's the way it was in the south.

CHAPTER 2

$\mathcal{W}$e were successfully working together to keep food on the table until one memorable Christmas Eve in 1950. It started out just like any other day. We got up around 5:30 am, ate breakfast and prepared our lunch for later. This was considered part of the job to get up early and pick up workers along the route…not that we were paid extra to do it, but that it was expected as part of the job. On that particular morning, some of the workers decided to pick up some "home brew." This was also referred to as "moon shine", "holiday cheer" and the like. Looking back, I guess they just wanted to get an early start getting into the Christmas spirit. No harm, so I thought…except that we were a few minutes late as a result.

Upon our arrival, Mr. Hershel Anderson, who was waiting for us in his Studebaker pickup truck got out and began yelling at my brother. "Nigger," he addressed my brother like that was his God-given name, "why were you late?" And before Eddie Jr. could open

19

his mouth to answer, he slapped him across the left side of his face. Now, a little background: we didn't have much, but we were a proud family. Everything we owned, we worked for. And since we had been removed from slavery, (albeit not very far removed) the thought of another man slapping the hell out of one of us in front of friend or foe did NOT sit well with anyone from our family. So much so, that his response was more of a reflex than a well-thought-out reaction…He punched Mr. Hershel, a white man, so hard he knocked him to the ground. When Mr. Hershel got up, he ran to his truck. Naturally, Eddie thought he was going to get his gun and ran off into the woods.

I was terrified for my brother and the rest of my family realizing what the Ku Klux Klan (KKK) could do to us. It was also well known that Mr. Anderson had been involved in several lynchings a couple years prior.

It was about that time also that my brother helped to organize a group of approximately 20 black men to join a union called the Wood Workers of America in an effort to negotiate a fairer wage. They were holding a secret meeting at a local church, but somehow the KKK found out about it and decided to discourage us from that. They came to the church with high powered rifles and shot it up! By the grace of God, no one was injured.

One of the most difficult decisions I had to make was to not follow my brother into the woods that day following his altercation with Mr. Hershel. But, I knew if I did, it was possible they might have found and killed both of us, leaving our family all alone in the midst of this terrible situation which had arisen.

In my mind, I was again reminded of the Wimbley brothers. Reportedly, a particular white man wanted to take over the Wimbleys' business. The brothers had established a pretty successful business cutting and hauling pulp wood. They were suddenly and inexplicably murdered; as they were later discovered with two rifles which had been planted alongside their bodies making it appear that they were the perpetrators and had been murdered in self-defense. There was no justice in the south those days. Not for a black man...the actual perpetrators never even went to trial for their crimes against the brothers. Instead, the Grand jury decided the brothers were killed in self-defense; leaving two more black families without a husband, father or provider...while the murderer set up shop with a prosperous pulp wood business that the Wimbley brothers had built.

Black-on-black crime was not even considered a crime. But if a black man were to attempt to defend himself against assault by a white man, that was considered a crime worthy of death.

After praying to the Lord about it for a minute, I decided to continue working for the rest of the day. "Surely", I thought, "Mr. Anderson would soon send out a search party which would have included dogs and Klansmen to seek quick and fatal retribution." That was the longest day of my life!

The next day was Christmas, and it is one I'll never forget. After coming home from working for the man who had just assaulted my brother, I had a bitter-sweet reunion with Eddie. Bitter, because I knew how much trouble he was in; sweet because he was alive! But I was very worried because Eddie was acting as if nothing had happened! It took, myself, a few of his friends and our cousins to convince him of the danger he had just put himself in. He had to leave town! And now!

We assembled a Posse together for the purpose of escorting Eddie out of town before he was killed. Armed with shotguns, we vowed to each other to open fire on anyone, regardless of who they were if they got in our way and attempted to prevent us. During that period, law enforcement officers were also a part of the Klan so they could not be trusted either. We were successful, however, and after a few days, returned home from Palmetto, Florida, Eddie's new home.

I tried to resume a normal life after returning home, working for the man who ran my older brother out of town. For four months, I managed to trudge through my daily routine for the sake of the family, but found it impossible to continue. He had promised that he would not have hurt my brother, but that did not make it any easier for me to work for him.

Now, it was entirely up to me to support my family. I tried unsuccessfully to keep my emotions in check and concealed, but to no effect. Alcohol would soon become my best friend as I tried to deal with the emotions as best I could; The pain brought on as a result of my brother being forced to leave town, the ensuing chaos, heartache, fear and uncertainty were just a few of those emotions. I know now I just was not mature enough at that time to be prepared to deal with that pain. At times, it seemed almost unbearable. I spent many a night crying myself to sleep...until one night, my mother heard me. She seemed to understand without saying a word the source of my pain. Finally, my mother (Mary) perceiving the pain I was going through, suggested I leave and go to be with my brother Eddie in Florida.

I wanted so much to be with my older brother, but I did not want to leave my mother and my remaining brothers and sisters Kenneth (KJ), Harold, Esther, Bernice, Sallie and Shirley. I had also found a new love interest in Annie Pearl who I had grown quite fond of that I had to consider also. But in the end, we made the tough decision to move away from home in an attempt to make a new and better home for all of us.

It was especially hard for me knowing there would be many hardships for my mother, sisters and brothers. KJ was the next eldest brother and he was only 14 years old. He would have to grow up fast because he was now the man of the family.

The first major decision KJ had to make was to move our family onto a sharecropping plantation to work. I know this was a difficult decision for Kenneth to make, but it was probably the only decision he could make so the family could survive. The situation was also complicated by the fact that we had owned our land prior, and were not used to working for anyone but ourselves.

According to Wikispaces and the Great Depression,

Sharecropping in the 1930's was as near to being a slave as you could become. After slavery was abolished, many of the lands that were once worked by black slaves were in need of a new work force. The land-owners then came across the prospect of sharecropping. The idea being that someone else could work all of their land and take 50% of what they made and keep it. This allowed the rich land owners to suppress the (for lack of a better term) serfs and peons that tilled the land and worked on it. They made only enough money to keep a house going and while the rich land owners did none of the work they took the excess money and pocketed it like interest so they were essentially being paid for the use of their land while not having to put any work into it. The land owner usually provided animals or tractors to work the land. This left the share-cropper with no tools to continue his trade elsewhere and forced them to rely on the grace of the landowner. The problem with this idea came when tractors or Cats were capable of doing the work of ten families and the families were evicted with nowhere to go. This is another case of big business coming in and taking over the work of families putting them out of jobs and into the ranks of the millions of unemployed.

KJ found these working conditions intolerable! The only relief he could find from the pressure was in the bottle of the moonshine he had just begun to peddle as a side living. Needless to say, this did not last long before he began to seek a way out. Not long after I would leave, KJ would find a way to follow as I soon discovered.

It should be noted here that what my father, KJ enjoyed drinking the most was moonshine. As a young man growing up, not real-izing why my father drank the way he did, or why he drank that "rot gut" stuff, I became resentful towards him. I had no idea how his past affected him. This revelation about my father would offer valuable insight into why he became the man he was and bring with it a respect and appreciation that I had heretofore struggled to attain. I cannot imagine the pressure that a 14-year-old kid would have felt with that kind of responsibility. At fourteen, all I had to worry about was going to school—the very thing he wanted more than anything but was not able to achieve.

CHAPTER 3

"*I* caught the bus that following Sunday headed for Palmetto Florida to be with my brother Eddie with my mother's blessing," Hycel explained. My big brother met me at the bus stop and took me to his residence. After a brief and emotional reunion, I went to his place to unpack and get a good night's rest.

The next day, I was introduced to a new line of work; picking oranges in an orange grove. This line of work added a new meaning to the term "manual labor." I had to climb long, unstable ladders to grab oranges from tall trees and place as many as I could into a large sack before retreating down this same long, unstable ladder while attempting to maintain my balance. Climb back up, pick and sack oranges, climb back down… and so on, and so on, and so on….

This process would continue until I became totally exhausted…, it didn't take me long before I became too exhausted to continue. I thought the work was hard at the sawmill until I began to do this work. I realized right away that this would not become my chosen lifetime profession.

After doing various jobs upon leaving the Orchard, we landed a "decent" job at Harley Packing House. The hourly pay was pretty good and would suffice until we could get to the "Promised Land."

Not long afterwards, we left Florida on the back of a migrant farm worker caravan. We were subcontracted to various farmers by the caravan owner. While we would earn a small wage, he would earn a percentage of what we harvested. Becoming a migrant farmer was what we believed at the time would be our ticket to greener pastures (in this instance it meant making it up north).

We earned very little money, however, especially considering the terrible working conditions we had to endure. The work itself was very arduous but as migrant worker, you soon got accustomed to the deplorable conditions because often, it was the only source of employment available. In order to maintain steady employment, some migrant workers would follow the harvesting seasons year after year from Florida to North Carolina and on to New York making stops in between wherever needed gathering various fruits and vegetables.

After a brief stay in Holly New York, we headed to Pittsburgh, Pennsylvania where we stayed with my Aunt Reathel. She was a Godsend, and helped us get back on our feet.

Some 50 years later, I realize what affects the hardships we experienced as young men had on my family. I personally would never forget how the premature death of my father in 1947 affected me, my mother, eight brothers and sisters. Subsequently, losing her two eldest sons who departed the South after that Christmas Eve incident. It may have forced my mother to become a stronger woman, but helped contribute to what was probably the most difficult time in her life.

Subsequently, I don't believe my brother Eddie ever got over being slapped and publicly humiliated on a Christmas Eve back in 1950. In my heart, I still believe that it had something to do with him dying at the young age of 51.

As mentioned, when Eddie and I left the South, the next oldest son in line who was left behind was Kenneth, otherwise known as KJ, also known as the father of my co-author Kenneth Bernard Peterson, his oldest son, and my nephew. He and all the children who remained and were old enough to work soon became share-croppers. KJ, in particular, underwent additional burdens as he attempted to help put food on the table—even dabbling in moon shining (helping produce illegal alcohol during prohibition). These stills were multiplying rapidly during this period in the south, and became an easy way to make a couple of bucks back then.

My younger sister Sallie once informed me of an incident involving KJ that gives me chills today when I think about it. Our mother was awakened one evening by a man who stopped by to request some assistance with a delivery from KJ. At the time, my mother was not aware that KJ was involved in moonshining. We were all aware, however, that she did not approve of the practice. Mama told KJ he couldn't go… Maybe she sensed something was not right. KJ would never disobey mama: no matter what. So, he refused to go. Later that night, this gentleman was found dismembered by the side of the road… apparently murdered!

My mother was a Godly woman—deeply spiritual and equally intuitive. Often, she would refer to the Holy Spirit as "leading her one way or the other." I credit her and her faith in God for helping us survive during those turbulent times. It was difficult enough to have to live in the south during that period, but nearly impossible trying to make it without a husband and a father to help take care of you, eight children and two aunts. Psalms 58:5(KJV) declares the Lord as a father of the fatherless and a judge and protector of widows. God became our source... And my mother's faith helped us get through it all.

After this incident, KJ left Georgia with nothing but a few dollars and a couple of outfits. The hand writing was on the wall for my brother. He and cousin Charles " Wincel" hitched a ride to Philadelphia, Pennsylvania with a couple who were headed back to Philadelphia after a short visit to family in the south. He left behind Mama, Bernice, Sallie Shirley and Harold. They continued to sharecrop until we were later reunited in Pittsburgh.

I had previously watched my brother Eddie leave the south under very similar circumstances. Young men made a practice of escaping the horrors of the South in that manner. It was risky business being young and black in Georgia during that time.

KJ and Cousin Wincel stayed in Philadelphia until my uncle Charles came and brought them to Pittsburgh. At first, I thought I had reached the promised land. It was the land of the free black man. I soon discovered that it was not all that I thought it would be. The areas of town where most of the blacks lived was full of sub-standard housing. Additionally, they were all crowded in the same small neighborhoods.

CHAPTER 4

*E*mployment for blacks in Pittsburgh usually involved the dirtiest and the lowest paying jobs available. Although not representative of equal opportunity, by comparison to what was available in either Florida or Georgia, it was much better. My first job was that of a counter attendant at a five and dime store. I was once taught as a young man by a much older and wiser man who lived next door to me. He said, "you don't quit a job until you have another to replace it." All my working life, I have had tried to heed that important advice. Often holding onto some of the jobs when it would seem way past the time to move on. I had always been taught that a half-a-loaf was better than none. At times though, it did seem like many of the jobs I took didn't even supply me with that. I have learned over the years to be grateful in little or to be grateful in much. As the Apostle Paul stated in Philippians 4:11 KJV, "Not that I speak in respect of want: for I have learned, in whatsoever state I am, therewith to be content."

Besides offering me good advice, another thing that I would learn to appreciate about my neighbors in Pittsburgh was that they would always look out for each other. Many would go out of their way to let you know of developing job opportunities which was how I came to work for this foundry in Pittsburgh. That was a decent job. I worked there until being drafted into the United States Army in 1953 and was discharged in 1955.

Hycel's Army Photo

I was drafted into the army through the local board in Cuthbert Georgia. Our first stop was Fort McPherson in Atlanta Georgia where we were sworn in and given what we call the "Flying 20"…

twenty dollars which we could use to purchase toiletries and cigarettes as we prepared for our tour of duty. Once again, we boarded the bus, but this time we were headed to Fort Jackson, South Carolina to be issued clothing, weapons etcetera. This experience was also where I received my first dose of military discipline.

The drill sergeant had informed us that the last man to come to attention, when coming into formation after dinner, would have a nice job waiting for him after duty hours. That happened to be me, as I was caught up in a game of pinball when I heard the whistle blow. Although I ran as fast as I could, it was not fast enough. I was placed on twenty-four-hour KP duty washing pots and pans and peeling potatoes. The moment it seemed I came to the end of a pot or a potato, the sergeant in charge would give me more. I learned a valuable lesson that day and was never late again during my two years in the Army.

From there, we went to Fort Sill Oklahoma where we received additional training. I was stationed there for two years from 1953 through 1955 (except for two months which I spent in Indiantown gap, Pennsylvania). This was an especially violent time in American history; with most of the violence directed towards blacks for asserting their rights to equal treatment under the law.

In effort to be treated as equals, and obtain civil rights, African-Americans endured beatings, were hosed like animals, attacked by

35

dogs and even murdered... All while I was fulfilling my vow to support and defend the Constitution of the United States against all enemies foreign and domestic.

This reminded me of a well-quoted statement by a once-famous cartoon character, pogo: "We have met the enemy, and he is us." Or an even more quoted passage which asks the rhetorical question, "Can a house divided against itself stand?"

It was difficult at best for me to fight for my country during these turbulent times. I watched helplessly as Blacks as a race of people were so badly mistreated while the government I was defending sat idly by.

It was also during this period that horrendous crimes were committed against any apparent leaders seeking to help right the wrongs that had been committed against African-Americans. Medgar Evers, a civil rights activist and Secretary for the of the NAACP in the 1950s, was assassinated during this period. Emmett Till, a 14-year-old boy from Chicago, was brutally beaten and murdered for reportedly flirting with a 21-year-old white woman.

Both of these atrocities occurred in Mississippi. It was hard to fight for my country during this time; however, I fought the fight as a good soldier to the best of my ability and achieved a rank of E-4 before leaving the Army. I managed to achieve the good conduct medal before I was honorably discharged from the United States Army in September of 1955.

I was glad to get back home to Pittsburgh, but it became all too clear not long afterwards that I would have some adjusting to do. Getting used to civilian life was not easy, and I partied a little too much once I got out. That's also when I met my wife Dezaree Bass who would later come to bear three children for me; Jacquelyn, Denise and Leon. (my daughter Denise would later die of lead poisoning at age 3).

Dezaree Bass (Peterson) Hycel's wife and mother of his children

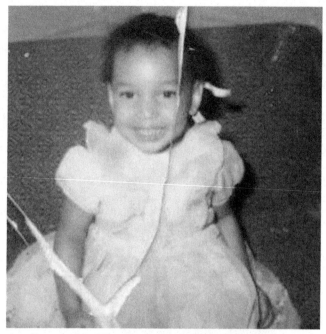

Jacquelyn Peterson Hycel's first daughter

Hycel Leon and Jacquelyn Peterson, Hycel's children

I also entered Masonry school (Technician Training School) about that time. It seemed to me at the time to be the best way to get a foot in the door to the industry I believed I had a calling to. School became just another avenue where discrimination, prejudice and unfair employment practices were also prevalent. Instructors did not seem willing to help you learn. Questions went unanswered and often ignored. This practice continued as I got out of school and attempted to enter the construction business. Until affirmative action became the law of the land, there was no such thing as "equal opportunity."

Tradesmen such as plumbers, carpenters, electricians, cement and brick masons had a very hard time getting employed. Unskilled laborers had it a little easier but the pay scale was significantly lower.

My brother KJ got hired as a laborer (carrier) on a federal housing project in the city. After a few weeks of proving himself, he became a scaffold builder. It was not long before he gained favor with the foreman and put a plug in for me knowing I had just completed masonry school and had gained some experience bricklaying in Pittsburgh and the surrounding communities.

As enthusiastic as he was about the prospect of my becoming a brick mason on the project he was working on, I did not wholeheartedly share his enthusiasm. Prior to graduation, I was informed by one of my instructors that due to the difficulties becoming a part of the union in Pittsburgh, I might have to leave the city to get a union card.

Kenneth's foreman told him to bring me in the next morning, and that there was a "good chance" that I would get hired. It was about 6am when we got together, had a cup of coffee and proceeded to the work site. He had already been working on the job for about an hour before he came and introduced me to the foreman. He seemed to be a very nice person as he went through all the formalities of an informal interview, but informed me although there were no positions available now, he would let my brother know when there were. He also informed me that I would have to join the union.

Now, I had been told by many individuals how hard it was to join the union in Pittsburgh. Honestly, it infuriated me to see these large projects with not many blacks on them. If there were black tradesmen on a job site in Pittsburgh, it was usually understood that they had managed to get into the union in some of the southern states such as Virginia, North Carolina, South Carolina and Georgia.

Three months after I left the Army, I got a job working as a laborer at American Bridge Company in Ambridge, Pennsylvania. The job was a blessing, and because my family who had remained in Georgia, would soon be moving to Pittsburgh, it was a timely

40

blessing. I was determined to impress my new employer—so much so, that I missed my last bus back home. Pittsburgh was about 16 to 18 miles from Ambridge.

I remember that night well because it took me four hours (from 2 AM to 6 AM) to get home. The temperature was about 8° in the middle of January. By the time I got home, I had no feeling left in my feet. Nevertheless, I was back on the job the next day, and on time. Thinking of my family and all the things they would need, kept me going with supernatural strength during some of the more trying times. When I had no strength of my own, God gave me his. "When I am weak, then am I strong." 2 Cor. 12:10 (KJV)

CHAPTER 5

I kept this job until I was laid off. After which, I became unemployed until February of 1964. At that time, I was referred by a friend who was working for the steel mill in Blawnox, Pennsylvania. This is a suburb to the north east of Pittsburgh. He had been working there for a few years as a core maker. At the time, he was the only black in that department. Blacks were just beginning to make modest gains in the workforce because it was about that time that President Kennedy had signed into law the Equal Opportunity Act.

Initially, I was put on the standard 30-day probation period required for all new hires. My first job there involved cleaning the sand from the castings. The work was difficult to say the least. My duties were to clean and chip away the sand residue on the molds after the molten steel which had been heated to a tempera-ture of 2800° had cooled and hardened in the molds and was later removed. The castings would remain red-hot after the mold was removed and during the chipping process.

Although we were given asbestos coats to wear while working with the steel, at times, the heat was nearly unbearable. Many days, I would be on the verge of passing out due to the heat. I used my family (at this time I had a wife and two children) as motivation to keep working amid the seemingly impossible situation. I knew I was being watched, and those watching would not hesitate to give me the heave ho if I showed any sign of weakness. I was still on probation and needed to make a good showing if I was to maintain any possibility of getting promoted out of that hell-hole.

Prior to the posting a brick mason position by the union, I spoke with the number two brick mason and was made aware of his upcoming retirement plans. I had an inside track, so I thought. He is the one who suggested I bid on this position. I had watched many who had gone before me take the easy way out... Simply give in to the system and accept the fact that a man of color is not going to be able to get the same rewards in exchange for the same work in this society. The general consensus was not to make waves. At least, that way, you could remain employed. I wanted more! I deserved more!

After all, I was a model employee—never missed a day of work, never late, always busy every second while on the job, and more than qualified for this position. Eager to bid on this opening, I rushed to get a bid sheet, filled it out and returned it to the personnel department. I waited to be interviewed for the job. One week went by, then two, and finally four weeks went by and I still hadn't heard anything. I went to the vice president of the union to inquire about my bid. He told me, "it hasn't been filled yet." I was beginning to get an uneasy feeling.

Two weeks later, I noticed a new guy come through my work site with a set of tools. I felt like someone had stabbed me in my heart with a hot dagger.

Somehow without a word, I knew this man had gotten the job I so desperately wanted. I struggled to understand the apparent injustice done to me... even trying to decipher the language in the union contract as it pertains my situation. The way I interpreted the contract, any union member had the right to submit a bid for an open position. Later, after the position had been posted, and no one was interested, then the job could be filled from the outside.

I finished the probationary period and was given a copy of the new contract to review. It would seem more appropriate if one would be given a copy of the contract prior to starting the job. In

45

the contract, I discovered one of the possible reasons we might not get a copy to review prior to completing the probationary period— it contained detailed information about the Equal Employment Opportunity Act signed into law by Pres. John F. Kennedy in 1972.

After complaining to the union, I was instructed by the vice president to file a grievance. The grievance was never addressed and, consequently, my complaint of unfair labor practices was never resolved. I soon sought help outside of the Union. A friend of mine referred me to the NAACP and the Urban League for help with my case.

I was advised to write a letter to the Equal Employment Opportunity Commission (EEOC) in Washington D.C. About two weeks later, I received a letter informing me that my complaint was being reviewed. In the meantime, back at the ranch, the word had gotten out that I was in touch with the EEOC. I was branded a troublemaker, and in addition to the dirty looks I received, I was also scolded by a fellow laborer who was also black. He told me, "You know, that position was for whites."

I was astonished! I was naively led to believe that once a person, no matter what race they were, joined the union, they became a part of the "brotherhood." This assumption could not be farther from the truth as I soon found out.

My workplace environment soon became unbearable to work. I spent many sleepless nights worried and frustrated by my situation. There was much corruption in the union, and the company knew about it, but would often look the other way. I was constantly worried that the union or company would find a way to get rid of me before my complaint was resolved.

Finally, I received another letter from the E.E.O.C. informing me of the validity of my complaint. I was then given a date and time to meet with a company representative to resolve this complaint. Of course, that was not the end of it. I soon became a target of an intentional campaign to discredit my working qualifications. Sometimes I was assigned the more dangerous tasks which often had nothing to do with my job title; such as the one incident which I was told by my foreman to unload the hazardous chemical silicon dioxide, also known as silica. It was commonly known that inhaling silica dust can lead to silicosis, bronchitis, or even cancer. I would ultimately refuse. It was within my right because that was not what I was hired to do.

Another example of the foreman trying to trip me up was when my boss asked me to estimate concrete based on the amount of brickwork needed for a particular job. I knew how to order concrete and told him my estimate was eight yards. He said, "I'm going to order seven and a half yards." Well, I knew It would be short and of course, it was. He never admitted he was wrong.

I could literally feel the hatred every time I would ask a laborer to bring certain materials so I could do my job. That was his job to bring me what I needed, but the looks I would get for meager requests such as that had become routine. They made it their business to let me know everyday I was not welcome there, and their mission was to get me to leave. The sad part was that I was good at what I did, and I knew it. What made it difficult for me was the fact that they knew it too, and didn't appreciate it.

After a while, it got to me—the stress, the games, the pressure, the hatred and the politics of it all. I decided to look for another job. I was married at the time, and had my daughter Jacquelyn who was just an infant. So, it was not possible to just quit and not have a means to provide for my family. I sent a bold letter to Honing Blocks Masonry headquartered in New Kensington, PA. It was there that I got referred to a job in Meriden, Connecticut.

In desperate need of a mental break, compounded by the fact that I had a family to provide for, I moved to Connecticut where I rented a room at the YMCA. The preceding mental stress continued to take its toll on me even after I got out of that horrendous situation. Eventually, after about three months, I had a nervous breakdown and had to be hospitalized for six months. To date, that memory is still bitter-sweet; as is represents the best of times and the worst of times for me.

The best part of that period was when I got out of the hospital. I didn't know it, but my wife had since relocated to Newark, NJ about 100 miles away from Meriden. My company, Nu-Towne Construction trusted me enough to make me foreman on the Sussex Mall construction project in Newark, NJ. One of my proudest accomplishments was over-shadowed by one of the darkest times in my life. I had significant responsibility on this large project; a promotion indeed!

Not everyone was happy about my new-found success as I soon discovered. Although most of the crew conducted themselves in a professional manner, there were some, who seemed to make it their personal mission to make my life as difficult as possible. My immediate supervisor was one of those people. Fortunately for me, one of the engineers witnessed some of his "discretionary" tactics and fired him on the spot.

I was diligent on this job, because I really wanted to make a good impression. So diligent, in fact, that I wasn't spending enough time with my family. As we were enjoying a moderate amount of success due to the new job, it created a lot of jealousy in the neighborhood. Some of the women helped to create additional tensions by inviting my wife out with them on occasion. On one such occasion, they convinced her to stay out all night and party with them. When she came home, there was a confrontation which led to our eventual separation.

CHAPTER 6

$\mathcal{A}$s I was seated in the main cabin on a jet traveling from New Jersey to Oakland, California, I began to reflect; I was on a one-way flight that was not a terribly turbulent flight; at least not on the plane. The turbulence was apparent within me as I anguished over the fact that my marriage was broken, and I was now going to be separated from my two young children (during that previous period my son Hycel (Leon) was born). I had just said goodbye to them at Newark airport and was emotionally a wreck. The realization was that I was not just separated from them, but separated as far as the east is from the west.

All I really knew about California, was that my sister Sallie lived there. She was my baby sister, but as we have always been close, invited me to make a fresh start where there seemed to be more opportunities particularly for blacks.

Although starting over is never easy, it was complicated by the fact that I was in a new town, without my family, no job and no money. Sallie helped me out tremendously until my unemployment kicked in.

It rained every day for a month when I first arrived in California. It seemed so appropriate at the time because of my down mood. After it stopped raining, fishing seemed to be good for a while. To ease the pain and loneliness I was experiencing, I spent a lot of time fishing with some cousins I became acquainted with. They would often accompany me at the lake. It was a meager attempt at best to replace the love of one's family, but it did help keep my mind occupied. Maybe that's why I love fishing so much today.

Hycel fishing in San Francisco Bay

Eventually, I was able to start looking for work in the masonry industry. Unfortunately, unlike the East Coast, there weren't too many brick buildings at that time. I did have some training in dry-wall construction, so I decided to seek employment in that field. I noticed some houses in my sister's neighborhood that were being rehabilitated so I walked over and asked for a job and was hired. My brother in law, John Stevenson, became my partner rehabbing older homes such as the kind with 12-foot ceilings. My contractor was very pleased with our work so we kept busy for some time. The unions weren't set up like anything I was accustomed to seeing on the East Coast. So, I had to begin the process all over again of how to get and remain gainfully employed.

You had to first obtain a work permit from the union hall. Then, after you found a job, you were instructed to report to the worksite without having to report back to a shop steward. Work was distributed by the "boss" as he saw fit without consulting your Union.

The work was assigned in a piecemeal fashion. It was what was commonly known as journeyman wages. For example: 60 seats of drywall were to be put up in an 18-hour shift. I knew this was going to mean trouble for me because that meant that I could be placed at the mercy of any boss who didn't like me for any reason. The unions, for what they were worth, provided little-to-no support for the average black man as well as other minorities… Nonetheless, it was better than nothing.

On the West Coast, however, those laws meant to protect our rights as employees proved almost non-existent. I was fired unjustly so many times, I lost count. I soon began to realize that I needed to get some appropriate training if I was going to be able to make a career change. I enrolled in Laney College for training to rehabilitate buildings. I became qualified to work without supervision after obtaining my license. Becoming a licensed professional also helped unlock some additional opportunities for me through networking as I met a man who needed some brickwork done (brickwork is my specialty) and afforded me my first big opportunity in California.

His name was "Big Sam." He helped me start my first company in the masonry business, Masonry Unlimited. He hired me "blind." By that I mean without having the benefit of seeing any of my previous work because I hadn't yet completed any work in California. I was hired on a provisional basis so that he could assess my skill level in brick masonry. After watching me for only several minutes, he was able to properly assess that I knew what I was doing. He told me, "You're hired!" We negotiated a very fair deal for him in order to get the door open for future opportunities.

That building, located on the corner of 46th and Shattuck Avenue in Oakland, California still stands today. It became the only source of advertising I ever needed for my business to take off. It was comprised of beautiful brick arch work and complicated masonry. Once completed, anytime someone wanted to see my work, I pointed them to Shattuck Avenue. Because the building was located on a main thoroughfare, it was often very busy with traffic. People admiring my work would often stop and get my number for prospective jobs. I've always believed a picture is worth a thousand words (and in this case and actual brick monument). Once I completed that building, I had two more jobs lined up. I took the larger of the two jobs offered, of course.

**Shattuck Ave Store in Oakland California.
First big job in California.**

The following pictures represent some of the work I completed in California. Most of it was done right in Oakland, California though. Two of my proudest accomplishments were achieved while helping to build, refurbish and restore two mansions: one for a gentleman by the name of Sioum Gebeyehou and another for a Mr. Asarat.

California Construction Projects

**His Cadillac "Sweet Pete" also his nickname
Hycel's pride and joy:**

Hycel's old neighborhood in Oakland

CHAPTER 7

I spent 27 years making my new home in California, a land that I had come to love despite the many challenges I had to face. But I decided to move back East afterwards, and moved back to Georgia, where I first called home. I remember the drive like it was yesterday. I played one song on the cassette player over and over. It was and still is my favorite song today-Order my steps by GMWA, Women of Worship:

Order my steps in Your word dear Lord,

lead me, guide me every day,

send Your anointing, Father I pray;

order my steps in Your word,

please, order my steps in Your word.

Humbly, I ask Thee to teach me Your will,

while You are working, help me be still,

Satan is busy, God is real;

order my steps in Your word,

please, order my steps in Your word.

Bridle my tongue let my words edify,

let the words of my mouth be acceptable in Thy sight,

take charge of my thoughts both day and night;

order my steps in Your word,

please order my steps in Your word.

I want to walk worthy,

my calling to fulfill.

Please order my steps Lord,

and I'll do Your blessed will.

The world is ever changing,

but You are still the same;

if You order my steps, I'll praise Your name.

Order my steps in Your word.

Order my tongue in Your word.

Guide my feet in Your word.

Wash my heart in Your word.

Show me how to walk in Your word.

Show me how to talk in Your word.

When I need a brand-new song to sing,

show me how to let Your praises ring,

in your word,

Please order my steps in Your word,

Please order my steps in Your word.

I want to walk worthy,

my calling to fulfill.

Please order my steps Lord,

and I'll do Your blessed will.

The world is ever changing,

but You are still the same;

if You order my steps, I'll praise Your name.

Please order my steps in Your word,

Please order my steps in Your word

It was a different Georgia than I recall as a boy. This state which once handed my family and I our eviction notice now looked like the land of milk and honey. I was there only a little while before I began building things in Georgia commencing with the firehouse which was located in Kennesaw Georgia.

firehouse in Kennesaw, Georgia

I was only there for about 4-5 months before I had to leave for Pittsburgh to see about "Mama" who had gotten sick. Along with my sister Sallie, I took care of her until she went home to be with the Lord in the fall of 2004. Sallie and I are all that remain of my brothers and sisters. And we will tell this story to all who will listen. Pittsburgh remains my home to this day, but after Mama passed,

70

Sallie went back to her home in California. Still close as ever, we talk on the phone nearly every day.

In conclusion, by the time this book is published, I will be 85 years old. David said and I concur, "I have been young and I have been old, but I have never seen the righteous forsaken nor his seed begging bread." (ps. 37:25). God has blessed me with many gifts I've been able to use in the construction industry not the least of which is masonry and brick laying. I have gained a sense of pride over the years through my many accomplishments, but I realize none of this would have been possible without God's help.

Regardless of my many tribulations, which Jesus told us we would have in this world, with every brick laid, God has also helped build my self-esteem. From my humble beginnings to the present I know I have been truly blessed with gifts which came from God. I am efficient in five trades; carpentry, drywall, plastering, brick masonry and cement finishing) although I wasn't afforded the opportunity to graduate from high school. I have built many structures most of which are still standing today in various parts of the country.

From remodeling a small grocery store on Liverpool St. in Pittsburgh to being the general foreman on the Sussex Mall near Newark, New Jersey. But, most of all, I have my health, strength and am in my right mind—I have a family that loves me as dearly as I love them. Psalms 37:3 reminds us that the footsteps of a good man (or woman) are ordered by the Lord. My life is a testimony that truly validates that scripture.

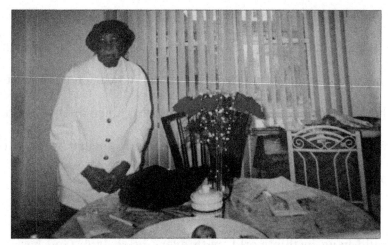

Mama

From left to right-cousins Walter Johnson, Alwin Peterson, Nedom Lowe and Hycel Peterson

**Hycel with girlfriend (and old flame)
Christine Matthews of Pittsburgh**

Hycel with niece Shelbra and daughter Jackie

**Hycel with nephew Tony, sister Sallie and nieces
Sasha and Janae**

**Hycel with daughter Jacquelyn and son Hycel Leon, great
grandson Jordan and granddaughter Jasmin.**

Generations! Father, daughter and grandson Juawan

Hycel with Mama and sister Sallie

(Insight from co-Author Kenneth Bernard Peterson)

As I stated in the beginning, I started working with my Uncle as a result of a desire to understand some of the Petersons' family history. This journey through my uncle's eyes has truly been fascinating. I will never take for granted what my ancestors had to endure so that I can enjoy the freedoms I have today. And with each family reunion I attend, I discover a little more about myself. For I also am a part of this village. I have learned because of my cousin Evelyn (Peterson) Peyton's research that my roots go way back to Africa in 1817. That is when a 4-year-old black male was taken from his country and sold to Thomas B. Peterson. He became a free man in 1863 and married Zerline Watts, a beautiful Mulatto woman and started his own family. They had seven children who lived to adulthood (affectionately known by family members as the "Magnificent Seven): Owen, Margaret, Sampson, Charles, Johnson, Richard and Zerline. They resided in Clay County, Georgia. Richard died on July 27, 1899.

(see Family tree below)

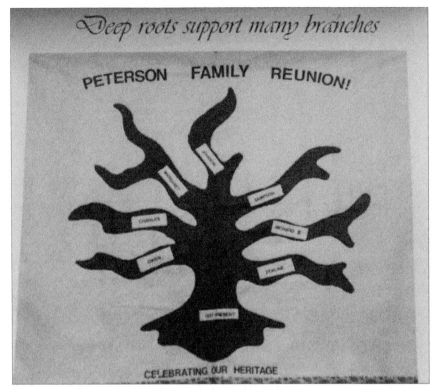

Peterson original Family tree

Uncle Hycel and I proudly hail from Charles. From that branch has sprouted many leaves and even more branches.

CPSIA information can be obtained
at www.ICGtesting.com
Printed in the USA
BVOW11s2113020817
490889BV00002B/9/P